The Flower Growers

The Flower Growers

Poems

Robert C. Jones

Robert C. Jones (signature)

THE MID-AMERICA PRESS, INC.
Warrensburg, Missouri

Cover and Section Designs
adapted from images of Monet from Editions Hazan;
Rilke from Crossing Cards; and van Gogh
from Vincent van Gogh Foundation

ISBN 0-910479-06-2

A Missouri Poets Publication

Financial assistance for this project has been provided
by the Missouri Arts Council, a state agency.

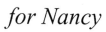

for Nancy

ACKNOWLEDGEMENTS

These poems, sometimes in earlier versions, first appeared in the following publications:

Ariel V: "Advice About Design."
Arlington Quarterly: "For T. S. Eliot."
Buffalo Spree Magazine: "For Johann Sebastian Bach: Suite No. 3 in D Major."
ByLine: "Advice From Basho," "For Robert Lowell," "Wood-Carver."
Chariton Review: "Three Chinese Paintings."
Christian Science Monitor: "Caryatid Collapsed Under the Weight of Her Stone," "Pablo Casals at Work," "Roses in Sunlight," "The Starry Night."
New Letters: "Delphi: Phaedriades."
Oblates: "The Circle of Summer."
Passage III: "*Celle Qui Fut la Belle Hëaulmiére.*"
Presbyterian Record: "For Ludwig van Beethoven."
Publications of the Missouri Philological Association: "Galway Kinnell Reads Poetry in Kansas City."
Sisters Today: "The Art of Listening," "Convergences," "The Olive Grove."

CONTENTS

The Flower Growers

I

"And those high prices one hears about, paid for work of
painters who are dead, and who were never paid
so much while they were alive, it is a kind of tulip trade,
under which the living painters suffer rather than gain any
benefit . . . . But one may reason that, though the tulip
trade has long been gone and is forgotten, the flower
growers have remained and will remain . . . ."
            —Vincent, to Anna van Gogh

THREE PROGRESS REPORTS FROM MONET

Brittany, 1886: "The sea
is giving me a terrible time of it. . . ,
so unlike the sea I'm used to painting. . . ."
The weather so changeable, dark wet rocks,
the green water against a leaden sky.
"I was quite unable to express its
intensity. . . ." *Rocks—grottoes, outcrops, needles—*
how to capture all this! "It's sinister
as hell, but quite superb. . . . I rage at my
inability to express it all
better." *And each day ending in rain. Strong*
tides, a devil of a wind, dark skies. "But
I have hopes of achieving what I want. . . ."

Rouen, 1893: "The further I get
the more difficult it is. . . ." *Mists, shadows,*
sunshine—each change in the quality
of the atmosphere is a new effect!
"More than ever I'm disgusted
by easy things that come in one go. "
Conveying the weather—painting
in rain and snow, trying to achieve that
"envelope above all"—the same light spread
over everything. "I tell myself that
anyone who claims he's finished a painting
is terribly arrogant."

Giverny, 1906. One constant cry:
"How difficult to paint! I can see what
I want to do quite clearly but I'm not
there yet!" *Always the rage:*
"You'd need to use both hands and cover hundreds
of canvases." *Always the wonder:* "What
lovely effects I was blind to in
the beginning. It's only now that I
can see what needs to be done and how. . . ." *And
the water lilies close before five o'clock.*

ADVICE ABOUT DESIGN

> *"I don't want to be interesting. I want to be good."*
> —Mies van der Rohe

At the Bauhaus, Gropius taught *truth*.
"Whatever conceals—
hides behind a curtain—
does not sing."

"One does not make a sonnet with ideas,"
said Mallarmé.
"One makes a sonnet with words."

(And Anna Sokolow told her dance class:
"Movements never lie.")

Mies van der Rohe learned
to make the line honest,
to show the grain of the wood.
Like a poet,
like a dancer:
Not be interesting—
be *good*.

PABLO CASALS AT WORK

After the portrait by Karsh

Rodin kept on repeating:
"Il faut toujours travailler!"
But the mute bronze figures,
the wash-drawings, the drypoint etchings—
they speak a different line:
form melodies
that echo still
in the empty studio,
the dark museum rooms.

The music of the heart,
Rilke might have whispered,
watching those fingers
move and mold and shape.

Pablo Casals, alone
there in the hall, must know
the same thrill of blood:
the dark gleaming cello alive
to the moving fingers,
the music spun
remembering
against the listening wall.

CARYATID COLLAPSED UNDER THE WEIGHT OF HER STONE

After Rodin

Her eyes, half-closed,
ask nothing.
Beneath the stone
too heavy for the slender neck
she waits—
endures the night—
unbroken.

BELOVED

Homage to Toni Morrison

Seven letters carved on dawn-colored stone—
and by and by all trace is gone: the dead
man on her face, the rubies of blood made
brighter by her midnight skin, her footprints.
Touch, if you like, but know: things will never
be the same. Forget where the memory
of the smile under her chin might have been
and was not. Forget the shadows still holding
hands on the way home, the circle of iron,
the loneliness, like a bad dream. Forget.
This is not a story to pass on. Love,
too thick to swallow, hurts. Anything dead
coming back to life hurts: Chokecherry tree,
tobacco tin where red heart used to be.
Forget. The rest is weather. Just weather.

THE AWAKENING

Homage to Kate Chopin

She could not have told why she was crying;
but a certain light was beginning to dawn
within her, the light which, showing the way
forbids it—like a mist passing across
her soul's summer day.
                              Ah! *si tu savais!*
The voices were like a discordant note.
"The bird must have strong wings," she remembered,
and kissed the cold glass passionately.
Shadows were creeping like grotesque monsters
across the grass. . . , *the beating of birds' wings,*
rising startled from the reeds, the faces
of the lovers, pale, drifting together—
but it was not love which had held this cup
to her lips. . . .
                      A bird with a broken wing
circled, disabled, down to the water.
Meeting and melting with the sky, the sea
reached out to enfold her in its embrace.
He, too, would melt out of her existence.
Her arms and legs were growing tired. *There was*
the hum of bees. . . musky odor of pinks.

RENAISSANCE PORTRAIT

Robed in cloth of gold
vestments—silent in a shell
of thought that circles like a wall—
he looks back at us. Trumpets speak: Bold
bright bells, their brazen voices fold
into the sky—and who's to tell
if those echoes please, or gall?
Cloud runs across sun. Cold
winds whip banners awry, quicken
marchers' steps. So. One last stand—
in this crowded square, unbroken
still by march of years—to find
comfort in vestments of stone,
hear music played for him, alone.

CHARLOTTE BRONTË AT HAWORTH

The wind cut deep
across the moorland,
the dark sky,
shaped heather into faces,
told the night.

The eager mouth
took stone.
The face became a mask.
Broken flowers,
shadow on the quarry pond.

The wind
followed the crooked street
to the churchyard.
Old words on broken stones.
Bone mask beneath the stone.

DELPHI: PHAEDRIADES

"The nameless uncarved block,"
Lao Tzu wrote, "is
but freedom from desire."
The shining ones at Delphi,
beneath the midday sun—
the stones of Delphi—
remember fire.

Water seeks out secret ways:
The mountain cleft, the sky.
The sky—a shout of angry blue
above the standing stones.

The shining ones at Delphi
stand,
stone beneath the sun.
The stone—
the nameless uncarved stone—
is warm
against the hand.

ENTRANCE TO A QUARRY

> *I was working on this when I felt the attack
> beginning.*
> —Vincent to Theo

You must stand up tall
when the wind sings
and stars fall
into the stone quarry.
The framework of the world
breaks through
and white sparks burn.
Green fire in the night sky.
Darkness
when I turn.

THE BLACK SWAN'S DREAM

Homage to Randall Jarrell

Again that harsh laugh echoed from the shore.
The sun stared through the reeds, a lonely face
with strange shuttered eyes that opened, closed,
and opened wide against the darkness, moon,
and stars. Ripples ran in and out of reeds,

the silky hairs of my wings sank like stones
on the rough lap of the wooden floor.
I heard, through the whispered steps of my feet,
my sister call. "Brother, you are dreaming."
I could not feel the lake, the night, the stars—

only the white stone wings, swimming, at last,
on the down of the pallet to the lap
and hiss of water, the laughter of frogs,
and far away, someone's *"Brother. . . brother,"*
like gentle hands, holding my troubled dream.

CELLE QUI FUT LA BELLE HËAULMÍERE

Homage to Rodin and Villon

Ah, Time, with treacherous wolves' teeth,
you have ravaged away my flesh.
I look at my naked body
and see my breasts poor and shrivelled.
What has become of my beauty—
the blonde hair, those lovely shoulders,
the dark-shadowed eyes whose bright glance
made all men my slaves and lovers?

Where's the long arms and dainty hands,
the full breasts, and hips, and firm thighs?
This is how human beauty goes:
My hair gray, my eyes turned yellow,
the shoulders thin and with a hump,
arms short, fingers stiff, and the thighs
no longer thighs but skin and bone—
a heap of mottled rag and flesh.

We poor old fools squat in our rooms
and think how we were in the past.
We clutch our blankets and complain
of the cold—we who used to be
aflame with youth and with hot blood.
And now that bright fire is put out.
All that's left—the taste of ashes.

But we used to be so pretty.

WALTZING ON VACI UTCA

November afternoon. A cold wind from
the Danube carries dead leaves and the lilt
of a Strauss waltz through central square.
Inside the broken circle of idlers,
shoppers, curious tourists, she sways
in three-quarter time to "The Lorelei."
Head tilted, raddled face turned to the sky,
she flirts with a shadow, smiles at the sun.
The cassette player, flanked by a basket
for coins, goes silent. Someone applauds.
She stoops, shoulders hunched, fumbles with the switch.
Again the tinny melody, again
the spinning, stumbling, steps along the street—
dead leaves, stirred by cold wind from the Danube.

IF THERE WERE DREAMS TO SELL

Gatsby. In that ridiculous mansion.
Throwing shirts—sheer linen and fine flannel
and thick silk—around the room. Daisy sobs,
"They're such beautiful shirts. It makes me
sad because I've never seen such—such
beautiful shirts before."

Like dreaming Bogart on Sesame Street.
He sings a little song, off key, and all
the usual kids push and shove around him.
He lights a cigarette, narrows his eyes
against the smoke, snarls, "G'wan. Scram!
That's all you get."

Like Dylan Thomas, filling the corner
of his hotel room with soiled shirts—a great heap,
worn once and thrown down. *Dylan, dreaming:*
tie loose, collar undone, cigarette drooping
from curled lips, smoke drifting up
into his half-closed eyes.

"NOT MARBLE NOR THE GILDED MONUMENTS"

Late Afternoon Thoughts
on Andrew Wyeth's Marsh Hawk

The hay wagons in this painting,
Andrew Wyeth wrote,
were "wonderful," the hubs and wheels
"magnificently constructed."
They dated back to around 1860.
Wyeth did the tempera on panel
in 1964—"some of my best drawing."
The marsh hawk sits on the fence
in the left distance.
Late afternoon light streaks across the field.
"The wagons," Wyeth said,
"were all swept away in a flood
down the river to Wilmington.
Nothing lasts. Shouldn't."

> *"Nothing lasts?"*
> *I look at the shape of the middle wagon,*
> *the way the front wheel*
> *catches the late afternoon light.*
> *Look at the marsh hawk waiting on the fence.*
> *Look one last time at the wheel of the wagon.*
> "Yes.
> Shouldn't."

GALWAY KINNELL READS POETRY
IN KANSAS CITY

1. At the Reading

"For this next poem," he said,
"I need another voice:
A singing voice."
The sleepy blue eyes pace the room.
"It's not difficult—really . . . .
Wouldn't someone. . . ?"
A scattering of handclaps.
Tall, black-haired, she steps toward the lectern,
looks back once.
"What's your name?"
"Kate."
"All right, Kate, let me just show you. . . . Here.
The singing isn't crucial.
What I want is loudness. You see?
Whatever embellishment you like—
but let it come out . . . big.
With volume."
When he tells her: "With volume,"
her left hand sweeps
her glasses from her eyes,
down—
simple as leaf-fall—
down to her side.

2. Parking Lot

Dead leaves blow through the parking lot
at the Raphael Hotel.
We lock the car and walk toward the bar.
Door slam.
A voice: "I don't believe this. Kinnell? Galway Kinnell?"
"Yes?"
"William Jay Smith."
"Of course! You're here . . . ?"
"To give a reading tomorrow. And you—?"
"I gave one tonight."
"Tomorrow?"
"I'm off to Columbia."
Wind tugs at our coats.
"This is how it must be all over the country—-
poets meeting in deserted parking lots at night."

3. Falling

Highway 50, moving across Missouri,
I think of starfish crossing their own bright mud.
Some dark stone strikes green fire in the sky,
burns its way down the windshield,
fades—silent, black. October leaves falling,
falling.

CONVERGENCES

Liquid crystal
that melody Johannes Brahms conceived
one day
and caught between the sheets of music manuscript
and his curling beard—
that Heifitz, poised and ice-serene,
spun in fine and web-drawn lines
the night I heard the wild geese overhead.
They came from the north,
trumpet voices falling
and echoing through the stars.

Long before the sun
I watched a comet
down the sky.
The wind breathed among the leaves.
I heard them—felt them—fall
in endless songs.

The comet, too, will fall
across the sun
and die.
I cannot hear its singing.
But its path is carved in crystal
where lines of wild geese fly.

ON THE ART OF THE FUGUE

I

Merely strike the right note at the right time—
just so! That still does not explain how carved
lines of sound dance together so they drift
(simple as golden ginkgo leaves drift home)
down time to find, at last, their destined form.
Johann, what deep mysteries you have left
us! We know only: Darkness came; you laughed
and made *flight* into resting place—a charm
against the night. Now we, each autumn, stand
and gauge *our* flight—a restless round, from spring
come once again to green the ginkgo leaf
against blue sky (as if gold never rained
last fall) to winter, turning through long, long
dreams to drift through time—remembering love.

II

The ginkgo tree, against the sun, casts long
shadows: dark echoes of the fires stars rained
last summer. Falling into sky, each leaf
recalls the pattern that it made in spring.
Galliard and allemande, gold dancers stand
and dance in air, advance, retreat, for love.
Just so, dear Bach, your music comes to charm
this night: dark sorrow soothed, bitter cares laughed
away—for each bright passage flown has left
us captured in its joy. This flight—this form—
this melody—you've turned it, brought it home
to play, transformed it, smiled, then let it drift,
at last, to rest as if, Johann, you'd carved
each note to fit its perfect place in time.

III

And so: the last note finds its way back home.
So we, out of our darkness, stir and drift
our ways toward light. The stream of music, carved
out of waiting silence, falls into time.
And we shall never make such golden form
nor wake such joyful dance of flight to charm
until we, too, remember how to laugh
at darkness, how to turn what light is left
into a song of praise. From fall of leaf
to willow green frenzy that harbors spring,
your notes still fly, Johann, although they stand
still: *raindrop echoes after it has rained—*
images of staring at sun too long—
love, once again, finding that home is love.

II

"In the end, those who were carried off early no longer
need us . . . . But we . . . could we exist without *them?*"
—Rainer Maria Rilke. *Duino Elegies*

POEMS TO RILKE

1

THE ART OF LISTENING

Trees saying over and over again
one same, same word, the still sun flowering
at dusk, the mouth of spring covered
with violets—the art of listening
is learned so slowly. What we ask the rose
has already found its answer in us, but we
must learn once again to hear it.

2

THIS SILENT, SEAMLESS WORLD

Like songs we once knew by heart, like voices
from our dreams, like sweet-salt taste of tears
long forgotten, this silent, seamless world
outgrows our grasp and we drop it, heedless,
into dark. Stars, perhaps, will remember
the leafless limbs of spring, the warm breath
of summer, the flower and fruit of autumn.
The wind, running through meadows, may pause
wondering if it has been here before.
The small trees we planted as children
have become too heavy to lift,
but we keep on trying to hold them firmly
in our simple hands, in our speechless hearts.

3

THE CIRCLE OF SUMMER

The rose pours into the circle of summer
a breath of blossoming trees.
Meadows let the wind go free.
The faded tapestry of sky
comes closer to the darkened houses.
Three starlings fly.
Like a cloud, the world keeps
changing its form. And the rose pours
into the circle of summer the same
breath of blossoming trees.

4

ROSES IN SUNLIGHT

do not speak summer only.
Their voices fill the garden
like held-in breath.
They tell us
what the sleeping rocks dream.

5

NOT DESIRE, BUT PRAISE

If song is reality, how can *we*
be real? Yes. Wedges of wild birds flying,
the ice shadow of the sky, the silent
walk of the moon, the world of clear water,
the voice of the sun—these pass through
sudden rightness. *Could* suffice. This world
is a kind of mirror; and in some strange way
we need each other. But true singing
is different—what the wind must hear
in that pure space where roses open
their eyelids. Not desire, but praise.

6

NOWHERE WILL WORLD BE BUT WITHIN US

Yes. *Nirgends wird Welt sein, als innen.*
Strange, now, to listen to words
that have forgotten you once spoke them,
see the rose, proud, tall-stemmed, loose its petals
on your unremembered mouth. When the star
falling heavenward gave you your life,
did you know, already, what we—who live
by perishing—must learn? When you sang of gardens,
did you know, even then, that memory
unfolds its bright flowers into darkness?
Once again we dance the ancient cycle,
slowly touch the sleeping seed to summer.
We do not know what part we play.
We do not know what we might awaken.

FOR ROBERT GRAVES AT THE WINTER SOLSTICE

Earth, air, fire, water; ground, sky, sun and sea.
There are no other stories, poems, or plays.
Altar breaks. Creed decays.
Axe will fell the sacred tree.
The hawk against the sky, the fox at kill.
The spider's venom raging still.
The ruined mask, the blooded blade.
These shadow-scattered plains,
no shelter from the bitter rains.
Broken towers upon a hill.
There are no other stories, poems, or plays.

FOR T.S. ELIOT

With what stumbling grace at last we live:
Rows of scattered markings on a page,
daubs of color,
fragments.
We create in blind majesty,
unknowing what we give.
The altars in the sacred wood
once burned.
Now, lost in sullen blood,
the leopard and the lamb both hide
behind this awkward mask,
sing to a discordant world—
child voices in the choir—
and grope for light they dare not ask.

FOR ROBERT LOWELL

> *"The corpse of the insect . . . prays that is*
> *perishable work live long enough . . . ."*

What if poetry didn't last?
Call it *May fly,*
choking on its own breath at mid-day.
Call it *milkweed,*
falling from itself—each moon-drawn word
spilling into the night.

Like a silver penny
it turns—
just beyond your fingertips—
a shining side,
a dark side.
A dark, lidless eye
you look into
at yourself.

FOR WALLACE STEVENS

A man skating
(the curl of the frozen shaving
that glides from the blade),
a woman combing
(the silk flow of softness)—
these, indeed, pass
through sudden rightness,
"will suffice."

Subtle mind:
to become that
which it has to find.

FOR LUDWIG VAN BEETHOVEN

May 7, 1824—Vienna

The world
ground to an ugly stop
and sound was a silent
scream inside his head.
Even then, he sang.
Broken bits
of anger, tears.
Even then,
he sang.

FOR JOHANN SEBASTIAN BACH: SUITE NO. 3 IN D MAJOR

If all light is turning—
as the sun turns in spirit—
here, in this dark chamber;
if all sound is music—
as whisper of movement,
arms bending and flowing—
here, in this dark chamber,
Johann, your inventions
turn players to flowers.
Each dark petal breathes,
opens and closes,
shadows of roses,
from touch into bloom—
as the hush in this room
follows music with silence.

III

"We hardly know life, we know so little of its foundation; and we are living in a period in which everybody seems to be talking raving nonsense, and everything seems to be in a tottering state. So it cannot be called being unhappy if we have found a duty that forces us to remain quietly in our corner, busy with our modest work . . . ."

—Vincent to Wilhelmina

LETTERS FROM VINCENT

1

SELF PORTRAIT

*"I keep looking more or less like a peasant. . .
and sometimes I imagine I also feel and think
like them . . . ."*
—Vincent to Theo

I have no ideas,
except to think that a field of wheat
is well worth the trouble
of looking at close up.
Summer is not easy
to express.
The great thing
is to give the sun
and the blue sky
their full force
and brilliance,
and the scorched fields
their delicate aroma
of thyme.

I should like to make
something of the cypresses,
they are always
occupying my thoughts.

2

THE OLIVE GROVE

"As far as the sorrow,
dear Mother. . . ,
which we have
and continue to have
in separation and loss. . ."
The limbs of the olive trees
are twisted.
"it seems to me it is instinctive,
that without that we could not
resign ourselves to separations. . ."
The leaves are like old silver
and silver turning to green
against the blue.
When the wind
touches them, they whisper.
"and that probably
it will help us to recognize
and find each other again later."
The orange-colored
ploughed earth waits
below . . . .

3

VILLAGE STREET

> *"I do my best to paint in such a way*
> *that my work will show up to good advantage*
> *in a kitchen . . . ."*
> —Vincent to Wilhelmina

Yellow flowers flow like sun bubbles
along the path.
On either side, the houses lean
toward one another,
old gossips
sharing the morning.
At the beginning of the sky,
one dark cypress stands,
gives shape to the tumbled red rooftops,
to the stairways going nowhere.

4

THE REAPER

> *"The study is all yellow, terribly thickly painted,*
> *but the subject is fine and simple."*
> —Vincent to Theo

The grain, scorched and tumbled,
the hills blue and green and brown
against a pale, fair yellow sky,
and this vague figure,
fighting like a devil
in the midst of the heat
to get to the end of
his task—
the image of death,
if you like.
But there's nothing sad
in this death.
It goes its way in broad daylight,
the sun flooding
everything
with a light of pure gold.

5

THE STARRY NIGHT

> *"One begins to see more and more clearly that life*
> *is only a kind of sowing time, and the harvest is not here."*
> —Vincent to Theo

In the salt-glazed night,
the kilns of stars
burn colors:
blue and green and red and gold.
On the crest of the hill,
a cypress shapes itself
against the wind,
unfolding into darkness.
Like a kind of flower
growing.

IN THE LAST YEARS OF THE TWENTIETH
CENTURY

In the last years of the tenth century,
work on many public buildings stopped in
expectation of the millenium.

But by '04, we are told, the workers went
back to the stones.   The Angel had not come.
Now, time grows short again—although we have
no instruments to measure time. Now, past
and present and future—all that was or
is or is to be—roll into one ball
inside the mind, each dreaming story complete
in us. The rains fall, the winds come, the years
revolve in the senseless circle of the earth
This time, what will the workers do? And what
will happen to the patient, uncarved stones?

ADVICE FROM BASHO

The world is a flower.
Enjoy the blossoms,
the scattering leaves.

The sky is a mirror.
Enjoy the reflections,
the woven straw shirt,
the carved wooden bowl.

Time is a dance.
Enjoy the seasons,
the moon and the snake,
the wind and the stone.
Enjoy the blossoms,
the dancing reflections.

Only the dance is sure.

THREE CHINESE PAINTINGS

1. Escaping the Summer Heat

Even light silk droops in the still air.
Brown earth is dull.
Come: In my green-shadowed pavilion—
cooling breezes.

We shall wear
robes of blue and gold.

2. Composing Poetry on a Spring Outing

Sunlight through leaves
makes gold damask on green grass,
brown earth.
The south wind! Small flowers,
tree, leaf-smell, bird song: All
here,
in this quiet circle
the eye composes.

3. Ink Bamboo

Paper imposes rhythm upon brush.
Brush sings against whiteness.
Whiteness becomes line, becomes leaf.
Leaf becomes shadow on paper.
Shadow on paper endures.

WOOD-CARVER

"You look for grain and texture," he said.
"Like walnut,
or this piece of quartered oak."
His fingers stroked the smooth surface.
"Not sapwood, mind you.
Heartwood is what you want.
You can tell by the darker color."
He picked it up, held it toward the light.
"And it needs to season.
Soaking in running water's best,
right after it's been cut.
Then you dry it out with wood smoke,
like the old carvers did.
There's pieces in English churches
must be five hundred years old,
still sweet and solid.
Took time." He nodded.
"Still takes time—
if you want to do it right."

GOLDBERG VARIATIONS

Bas reliefs dance down the walls
of the Franz Liszt Academy Auditorium.
Art Deco swans swim above the soft light
of candelabras held by Egyptian maidens.
Bach tonight. A Hungarian prodigy—
in a tuxedo too large—
bends over the keys, nods his head twice
in time to some invisible metronome,
spins out that thirty-two note sarabande:
Music with no beginning and no end.
"Ich bin so lang nicht bei dir gewest"
fading to silence. With no beginning
and no end . . . .

Robert C. Jones

From 1961 until he retired in 1991, Robert C. Jones taught in the Department of English and Philosophy, Central Missouri State University. In 1982-83, he was Senior American Fulbright Lecturer in American Literature, University of Timisoara, Timisoara, Romania; in Fall 1984, he was Resident Director for The Missouri London Program, an international enrichment program administered by a consortium of Missouri Universities and Colleges; in 1986-87, he was Visiting Fulbright Lecturer in American Literature, Aristotle University, Thessaloniki, Greece; in Fall 1989, he was Visiting Professor of American Literature at the University of Economic Sciences, Budapest, Hungary. Since 1997, he has been a presenter of "Missouri Writers: Their Gift to the Nation," for the Missouri Humanities Council Speakers Bureau. Currently, he writes and publishes poetry and occasional reviews; and he gives readings and poetry workshops for schools, writers conferences, and young authors conferences throughout Missouri.